MUSIC NOTEBOOK

Name ______________________________

Phone ______________________________

Made in the USA
Monee, IL
28 October 2025

33190484R00072